101 THINGS THE DEVIL CAN'T DO

Also by Maisie Sparks

101 Things God Can't Do

101 THINGS THE DEVIL CAN'T DO

What You Must Know to Win

Maisie Sparks

THOMAS NELSON PUBLISHERS®
Nashville

ACKNOWLEDGMENTS

My thanks and appreciation go to every pastor, teacher, missionary, evangelist, friend, and family member who caused a prevailing faith to seize my life.

May you continue to encourage others, and may you forever victoriously stand against all threats and attacks to your confidence in and love of God.

And this is the victory that has overcome the world—our faith.

I John 5:4

1. The Enemy can't win.

But thanks be to God, who gives us the victory through our Lord Jesus Christ.
I Corinthians 15:57

2. The Adversary can't have you.

Satan has asked for you, that he may sift you as wheat. But I have prayed for you, that your faith should not fail; and when you have returned to Me, strengthen your brethren.

LUKE 22:31–32

3.

The Accuser can't touch you without God's permission.

And the LORD said to Satan, "Behold, all that he has is in your power; only do not lay a hand on his person."

JOB 1:12

4. The Foe can't keep you fearful.

The LORD is my light and my salvation;
Whom shall I fear?
The LORD is the strength of my life;
Of whom shall I be afraid?
PSALM 27:1

5.

The Defiant can't dwell in heaven.

Therefore I cast you as a profane thing
Out of the mountain of God;
And I destroyed you, O covering cherub,
From the midst of the fiery stones.
EZEKIEL 28:16

6.

The Discourager can't keep you depressed.

Why are you cast down, O my soul?
And why are you disquieted within me?
Hope in God;
For I shall yet praise Him,
The help of my countenance and my God.
PSALM 42:11

7. The Dethroned can't be in charge.

For the kingdom is the LORD's,
And He rules over the nations.
PSALM 22:28

8. The Disobedient can't demand your obedience.

Do you not know that to whom you present yourselves slaves to obey, you are that one's slaves whom you obey, whether of sin leading to death, or of obedience leading to righteousness?

ROMANS 6:16

9. The Mistreatment can't get you down.

We are hard-pressed on every side, yet not crushed; we are perplexed, but not in despair; persecuted, but not forsaken; struck down, but not destroyed.
II CORINTHIANS 4:8–9

10. The Whipped can't demand to be worshiped.

Then Jesus said to him, "Away with you, Satan! For it is written, 'You shall worship the LORD your God, and Him only you shall serve.'"
MATTHEW 4:10

11. The Predator can't miss the bottomless pit.

He laid hold of the dragon, that serpent of old, who is the Devil and Satan, and bound him for a thousand years; and he cast him into the bottomless pit.

REVELATION 20:2–3

12. The Burglar can't find the source of your life.

For you died, and your life is hidden with Christ in God.

COLOSSIANS 3:3

13. The Arsonist can't beat the heat.

The devil, who deceived them, was cast into the lake of fire and brimstone where the beast and the false prophet are.

Revelation 20:10

14. The Fiend can't be your friend.

For what fellowship has righteousness with lawlessness? And what communion has light with darkness?
II CORINTHIANS 6:14

15. The Stranger can't be followed.

Yet they will by no means follow a stranger, but will flee from him, for they do not know the voice of strangers.
JOHN 10:5

16. The Devil can't have authority over you.

Behold, I give you the authority to trample on serpents and scorpions, and over all the power of the enemy, and nothing shall by any means hurt you.
LUKE 10:19

17. The Wicked can't be loved.

You who love the LORD, hate evil!
He preserves the souls of His saints;
He delivers them out of the hand of the wicked.
PSALM 97:10

18. The Snake can't beat even though he bites.

And I will put enmity
Between you and the woman,
And between your seed and her Seed;
He shall bruise your head,
And you shall bruise His heel.
GENESIS 3:15

19. The Cheapskate can't own you any longer.

For you were bought at a price; therefore glorify God in your body and in your spirit, which are God's.

I CORINTHIANS 6:20

20. The Scoundrel can't stand your submission to God.

Therefore submit to God. Resist the devil and he will flee from you.
JAMES 4:7

21. The Troublemaker can't be up to anything good.

Be sober, be vigilant; because your adversary the devil walks about like a roaring lion, seeking whom he may devour.
I Peter 5:8

22. The Bad Memory can't mess up your future because of your past.

But one thing I do, forgetting those things which are behind and reaching forward to those things which are ahead, I press toward the goal for the prize of the upward call of God in Christ Jesus.
PHILIPPIANS 3:13–14

23. The Slave Master can't put you back in bondage.

Stand fast therefore in the liberty by which Christ has made us free, and do not be entangled again with a yoke of bondage.
GALATIANS 5:1

24. The Impostor can't disguise himself from God.

Get behind Me, Satan! For you are not mindful of the things of God, but the things of men.
Mark 8:33

25. The Pest can't keep bothering you.

The LORD has broken the staff of the wicked,
The scepter of the rulers;
He who struck the people in wrath with a
*   continual stroke,*
He who ruled the nations in anger,
Is persecuted and no one hinders.
The whole earth is at rest and quiet;
They break forth into singing.
ISAIAH 14:5–7

26. The Imp can't make you subject to him.

Then the seventy returned with joy, saying, "Lord, even the demons are subject to us in Your name."
LUKE 10:17

27. The Con Man can't outsmart you.

The enemy shall not outwit him,
Nor the son of wickedness afflict him.
PSALM 89:22

28. The Proud can't stay on top.

How you are fallen from heaven,
O Lucifer, son of the morning!
How you are cut down to the ground,
You who weakened the nations!
Isaiah 14:12

29. The Intruder can't surprise you.

Do not be afraid of sudden terror,
Nor of trouble from the wicked when it comes;
For the LORD will be your confidence,
And will keep your foot from being caught.
PROVERBS 3:25–26

30. The Bad Habit can't ruin your life anymore.

For sin shall not have dominion over you, for you are not under law but under grace.
ROMANS 6:14

31. The Pimp can't give you your true worth.

For the wages of sin is death, but the gift of God is eternal life in Christ Jesus our Lord.
ROMANS 6:23

32. The Madman can't have a place in your life.

Do not let the sun go down on your wrath, nor give place to the devil.
Ephesians 4:26–27

33. The Liar can't tell the truth.

When he speaks a lie, he speaks from his own resources, for he is a liar and the father of it.
JOHN 8:44

34. The Horror can't last forever.

I cast you to the ground,
I laid you before kings,
That they might gaze at you . . .
All who knew you among the peoples are
    astonished at you;
You have become a horror,
And shall be no more forever.
EZEKIEL 28:17, 19

35. The Resentful can't imagine how much God loves you.

What is man that You are mindful of him,
And the son of man that You visit him?
For You have made him a little lower than the angels,
And You have crowned him with glory and honor.
You have made him to have dominion over the works of
Your hands;
You have put all things under his feet.
PSALM 8:4–6

36. The Demon can't doubt the reality of God.

You believe that there is one God. You do well. Even the demons believe—and tremble!

JAMES 2:19

37. Satan can't get God's glory.

Salvation and glory and honor and power belong to the Lord our God!
REVELATION 19:1

38. The Filth can't be allowed to do his dirty work forever.

And the God of peace will crush Satan under your feet shortly.
ROMANS 16:20

39. The Segregationist can't divide us.

Now whom you forgive anything, I also forgive. For if indeed I have forgiven anything, I have forgiven that one for your sakes in the presence of Christ, lest Satan should take advantage of us; for we are not ignorant of his devices.

II CORINTHIANS 2:10–11

40. The Fraud can't show you who he really is.

For Satan himself transforms himself into an angel of light. Therefore it is no great thing if his ministers also transform themselves into ministers of righteousness, whose end will be according to their works.
II Corinthians 11:14–15

41. The Hired Gun can't do his own thing.

And lest I should be exalted above measure by the abundance of the revelations, a thorn in the flesh was given to me, a messenger of Satan to buffet me, lest I be exalted above measure.

II CORINTHIANS 12:7

42. The Distraction can't stop God's plan.

Therefore we wanted to come to you—even I, Paul, time and again—but Satan hindered us . . . We thought it good to be left in Athens alone, and sent Timothy, our brother and minister of God, and our fellow laborer in the gospel of Christ, to establish you and encourage you concerning your faith, that no one should be shaken by these afflictions.

I Thessalonians 2:18, 3:1–3

43. The Grim Reaper can't keep you forever.

I am He who lives, and was dead, and behold, I am alive forevermore. Amen. And I have the keys of Hades and of Death.
REVELATION 1:18

44. The Sneak can't hide from God.

For the eyes of the LORD run to and fro throughout the whole earth, to show Himself strong on behalf of those whose heart is loyal to Him.
II Chronicles 16:9

45. The Deceiver can't change his destiny.

So the great dragon was cast out, that serpent of old, called the Devil and Satan, who deceives the whole world; he was cast to the earth, and his angels were cast out with him.

Revelation 12:9

46. The Seducer can't keep his promises.

Then the serpent said to the woman, ". . . In the day you eat of it your eyes will be opened, and you will be like God."

GENESIS 3:4–5

47. The Hypocrite can't keep you out of your Father's house.

*I would rather be a doorkeeper in the house of my God
Than dwell in the tents of wickedness.*
PSALM 84:10

48. The Rogue's mission can't change.

The thief does not come except to steal, and to kill, and to destroy. I have come that they may have life, and that they may have it more abundantly.
JOHN 10:10

49. The Tyrant can't make you tremble anymore.

Those who see you will gaze at you,
And consider you, saying:
"Is this the man who made the earth tremble,
Who shook kingdoms,
Who made the world as a wilderness
And destroyed its cities . . . ?"
Isaiah 14:16–17

50. The Archenemy's kingdom can't stand up to the kingdom of God.

And from the days of John the Baptist until now the kingdom of heaven suffers violence, and the violent take it by force.

MATTHEW 11:12

51. The Cunning One can't be blessed.

So the LORD God said to the serpent:
"Because you have done this,
You are cursed more than all cattle,
And more than every beast of the field."
GENESIS 3:14

52. The Invader can't penetrate your shield.

Above all, taking the shield of faith with which you will be able to quench all the fiery darts of the wicked one.

Ephesians 6:16

53. The False One has fallen and he can't get up.

And He said to them, "I saw Satan fall like lightning from heaven."
LUKE 10:18

54. The Tormentor can't hinder your rejoicing.

Beloved, do not think it strange concerning the fiery trial which is to try you, as though some strange thing happened to you; but rejoice to the extent that you partake of Christ's sufferings, that when His glory is revealed, you may also be glad with exceeding joy.
I Peter 4:12–13

55. The Villain's plans against you can't succeed.

"No weapon formed against you shall prosper,
And every tongue which rises against you in judgment
You shall condemn.
This is the heritage of the servants of the LORD,
And their righteousness is from Me,"
Says the LORD.
ISAIAH 54:17

56. The Tempter's temptations can't be unbearable.

No temptation has overtaken you except such as is common to man; but God is faithful, who will not allow you to be tempted beyond what you are able, but with the temptation will also make the way of escape, that you may be able to bear it.

I Corinthians 10:13

57. The Critic can't make you feel guilty anymore.

There is therefore now no condemnation to those who are in Christ Jesus, who do not walk according to the flesh, but according to the Spirit.

ROMANS 8:1

58. The Attacker and his accomplices can't outnumber you.

Do not fear, for those who are with us are more than those who are with them.
II Kings 6:16

59. The Lawless can't defeat you.

The LORD will cause your enemies who rise against you to be defeated before your face; they shall come out against you one way and flee before you seven ways.
DEUTERONOMY 28:7

60. The Traitor can't triumph over you.

By this I know that You are well pleased with me,
Because my enemy does not triumph over me.
PSALM 41:11

61.   The Fake can't shake you from your firm foundation.

Cast your burden on the LORD,
And He shall sustain you;
He shall never permit the righteous to be moved.
PSALM 55:22

62. The Devourer can't consume you.

You shall not be afraid of the terror by night,
Nor of the arrow that flies by day,
Nor of the pestilence that walks in darkness,
Nor of the destruction that lays waste at noonday.
A thousand may fall at your side,
And ten thousand at your right hand;
But it shall not come near you.
Psalm 91:5–7

63. The Creep can't be trusted.

Then the serpent said to the woman, "You will not surely die."
GENESIS 3:4

64. The Wretch's works can't be defended.

For this purpose the Son of God was manifested, that He might destroy the works of the devil.
I JOHN 3:8

65. The Terminator can't stop God's purpose for your life.

And we know that all things work together for good to those who love God, to those who are the called according to His purpose.
ROMANS 8:28

66. The Slanderer can't curse you.

Then Balak said to Balaam, "What have you done to me? I took you to curse my enemies, and look, you have blessed them bountifully!"
NUMBERS 23:11

67. The Defeated can't defeat you.

Yet in all these things we are more than conquerors through Him who loved us.

ROMANS 8:37

68. The Trial can't trouble your joy.

My brethren, count it all joy when you fall into various trials, knowing that the testing of your faith produces patience. But let patience have its perfect work, that you may be perfect and complete, lacking nothing.
JAMES 1:2–4

69. The Nemesis can't stay when you use the Word.

But He answered and said, "It is written, . . ."
Jesus said to him, "It is written again, . . ."
Then Jesus said to him, " . . .
For it is written, . . ."
Then the devil left Him, and behold,
angels came and ministered to Him.
Matthew 4:4, 7, 10, 11

70. The Finger Pointer can't destroy a righteous reputation.

Then the LORD said to Satan, "Have you considered My servant Job, that there is none like him on the earth, a blameless and upright man, one who fears God and shuns evil?"

JOB 1:8

71. The Scorner can't stop you from praising God.

Let the redeemed of the LORD say so,
Whom He has redeemed from the hand of the enemy.
PSALM 107:2

72. The Big Bully can't intimidate you.

You come to me with a sword, with a spear, and with a javelin. But I come to you in the name of the LORD of hosts, the God of the armies of Israel, whom you have defied.
I Samuel 17:45

73. The Crook can't steal your peace.

When a man's ways please the LORD,
He makes even his enemies to be at peace with him.
PROVERBS 16:7

74. The Gangbanger can't overwhelm you.

When the enemy comes in like a flood,
The Spirit of the LORD will lift
up a standard against him.
ISAIAH 59:19

75. The Nobody can't mean anything to you.

Those who war against you
Shall be as nothing,
As a nonexistent thing.
ISAIAH 41:12

76. The Abuser can't understand how you stand it.

For our light affliction, which is but for a moment, is working for us a far more exceeding and eternal weight of glory, while we do not look at the things which are seen, but at the things which are not seen. For the things which are seen are temporary, but the things which are not seen are eternal.

II CORINTHIANS 4:17–18

77. The Doubter can't quench your faith.

For I know whom I have believed and am persuaded that He is able to keep what I have committed to Him until that Day.
II TIMOTHY 1:12

78. The Schemer's strategies can't work.

And the Lord will deliver me from every evil work and preserve me for His heavenly kingdom.
II Timothy 4:18

79. The Jealous can't stop what God has for you.

You prepare a table before me in the presence of my enemies;
You anoint my head with oil;
My cup runs over.
PSALM 23:5

80. The Predator can't get to you.

The angel of the LORD encamps
  all around those who fear Him,
And delivers them.
PSALM 34:7

81. The Abductor can't take you anywhere God can't go.

*Yea, though I walk through the valley
of the shadow of death,
I will fear no evil;
For You are with me;
Your rod and Your staff, they comfort me.*
PSALM 23:4

82. The Brute can't be as big as he looks.

You are of God, little children, and have overcome them, because He who is in you is greater than he who is in the world.

I John 4:4

83. The Covetous can't ever get what he wants.

For you have said in your heart:
"I will ascend into heaven,
I will exalt my throne above the stars of God;
I will also sit on the mount of the congregation . . .
Yet you shall be brought down to Sheol,
To the lowest depths of the Pit."
Isaiah 14:13, 15

84. The Disarmed can't overpower you.

Having disarmed principalities and powers, He made a public spectacle of them, triumphing over them in it.
COLOSSIANS 2:15

85. The Difficulty can't make you doubt God.

Though He slay me, yet will I trust Him.
Job 13:15

86. The Condemned can't condemn you.

Who shall bring a charge against God's elect?
It is God who justifies. Who is he who condemns? It is
Christ who died, and furthermore is also risen, who is
even at the right hand of God, who also makes
intercession for us.

Romans 8:33–34

87. The Rebel can't beat your Commander.

For the LORD your God is He who goes with you, to fight for you against your enemies, to save you.
DEUTERONOMY 20:4

88. The Corrupted can't get from under God's feet.

Through God we will do valiantly,
For it is He who shall tread down our enemies.
PSALM 60:12

89. The Fire can't cool your faith in God.

Our God whom we serve is able to deliver us from the burning fiery furnace, and He will deliver us from your hand, O king. But if not, let it be known to you, O king, that we do not serve your gods, nor will we worship the gold image which you have set up.
DANIEL 3:17–18

90. The Intimidator's threat of death can't frighten you any longer.

Blessed are the dead who die in the Lord from now on. "Yes," says the Spirit, "that they may rest from their labors, and their works follow them."
Revelation 14:13

91.
The Corrupt can't have a happy ending.

And they will be tormented
day and night forever and ever.
REVELATION 20:10

92. The Molester can't hold on to you.

"But I will deliver you in that day," says the LORD, "and you shall not be given into the hand of the men of whom you are afraid. For I will surely deliver you, and you shall not fall by the sword; but your life shall be as a prize to you, because you have put your trust in Me," says the LORD.

JEREMIAH 39:17–18

93. The Taskmaster can't make you a slave to fear.

For you did not receive the spirit of bondage again to fear, but you received the Spirit of adoption by whom we cry out, "Abba, Father."
ROMANS 8:15

94. The Unrighteous can't be your master now.

But God be thanked that though you were slaves of sin, yet you obeyed from the heart that form of doctrine to which you were delivered. And having been set free from sin, you became slaves of righteousness.
ROMANS 6:17–18

95. The Dirt can't keep you down.

Do not rejoice over me, my enemy;
When I fall, I will arise;
When I sit in darkness,
The LORD will be a light to me.
MICAH 7:8

96. The Wicked's weapons can't beat yours.

For the weapons of our warfare are not carnal but mighty in God for pulling down strongholds, casting down arguments and every high thing that exalts itself against the knowledge of God, bringing every thought into captivity to the obedience of Christ.
II CORINTHIANS 10:4–5

97.

The Lunatic can't keep you from fasting and prayer.

However, this kind does not go out except by prayer and fasting.
Matthew 17:21

98. The Evil One can't have authority over your life's mission.

And Jesus came and spoke to them, saying, "All authority has been given to Me in heaven and on earth. Go therefore and make disciples of all the nations, baptizing them in the name of the Father and of the Son and of the Holy Spirit, teaching them to observe all things that I have commanded you; and lo, I am with you always, even to the end of the age." Amen.
Matthew 28:18–20

99. The Nut can't make you crazy.

And the peace of God, which surpasses all understanding, will guard your hearts and minds through Christ Jesus.
Philippians 4:7

100. The Trickster can't penetrate godly armor.

Finally, my brethren, be strong in the Lord and in the power of His might. Put on the whole armor of God, that you may be able to stand against the wiles of the devil.

Ephesians 6:10–11

101. The Antagonist can't beat you out of your reward.

I have fought the good fight, I have finished the race, I have kept the faith. Finally, there is laid up for me the crown of righteousness, which the Lord, the righteous Judge, will give to me on that Day, and not to me only but also to all who have loved His appearing.
II TIMOTHY 4:7–8

About the Author

As a member of the Apostolic Faith Church on Chicago's south side, Maisie Sparks has a long history of contributing to Christian publishing. She has published *The Transformer,* a newsletter for new believers, and serves as editor for publications of the International Pentecostal Young People's Union.

Sparks and her husband, James, live in Chicago with their two sons, Philip and Andrew.